Math = Fun

Adding Fractions

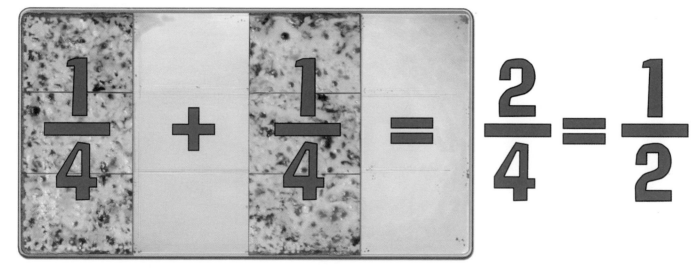

$$\frac{1}{4} + \frac{1}{4} = \frac{2}{4} = \frac{1}{2}$$

by Jerry Pallotta
Illustrated by Rob Bolster

SCHOLASTIC INC.

New York   Toronto   London   Auckland   Sydney
Mexico City   New Delhi   Hong Kong   Buenos Aires

To Santarpio's Pizza of East Boston, the best pizza in America.
I'll have a double garlic with anchovies, thank you!
—*Jerry Pallotta*

To Gennaro Lombardi, who in 1905 opened the first American pizzeria in New York City.
—*Rob Bolster*

Text copyright © 2008 by Jerry Pallotta.
Illustrations copyright © 2008 by Rob Bolster.
All rights reserved. Published by Scholastic Inc.
SCHOLASTIC, Math = Fun!, and associated logos
are trademarks of Scholastic Inc.

ISBN-13: 978-0-439-92349-1
ISBN-10: 0-439-92349-2

12 11 10 9 8 7 6 5 4 3   8 9 10 11 12 13/0

Printed in the U.S.A.
First printing, January 2008

What is a fraction? A fraction is a part or a portion of a whole thing.
Let's learn how to add fractions!
First, start with a delicious pizza.
We will cut it into twelve equal slices.

We thought of using a bicycle instead of a pizza.
But taking a bicycle apart leaves you with unequal pieces.
It won't work.

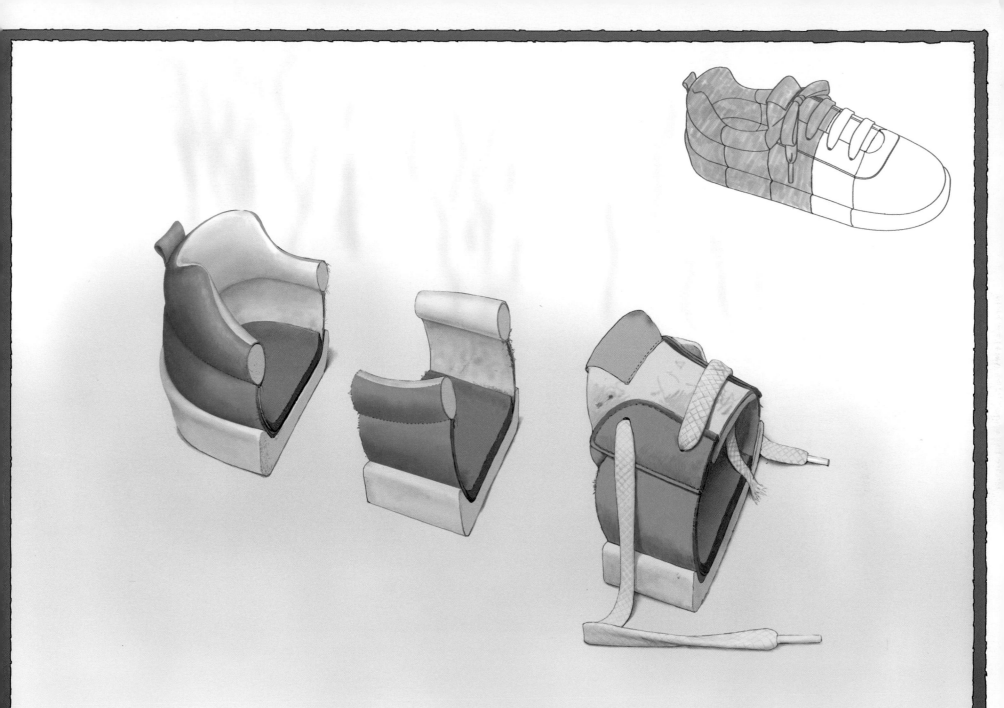

For fun, we tried using a sneaker.
Teachers and parents might not like working with sneakers;
it could lead to smelly math.

Pizza!

Back to the pizza! We are cutting it into twelve equal slices.

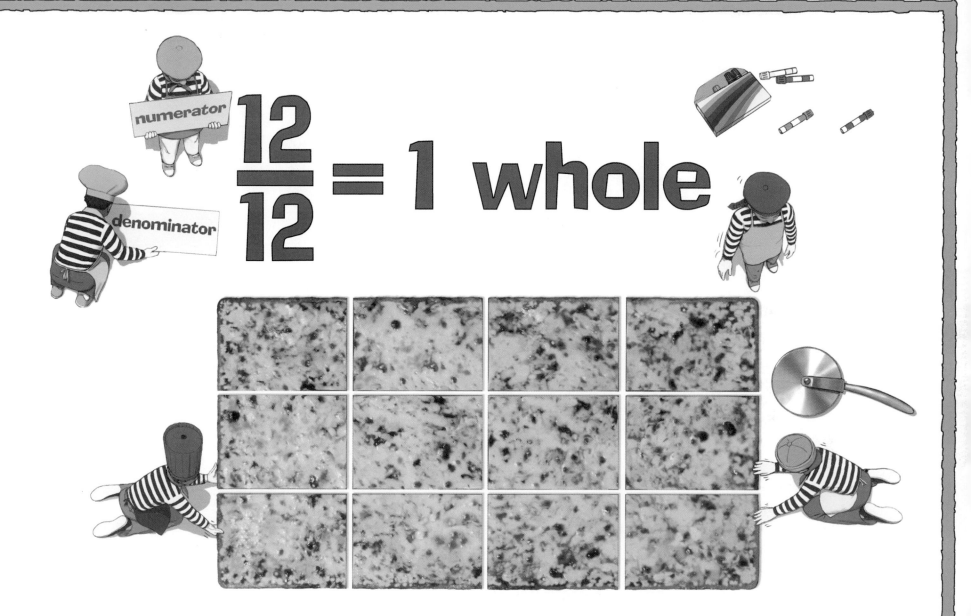

$$\frac{12}{12} = 1 \text{ whole}$$

numerator

denominator

Now we have a twelve-slice pizza.
There are twelve equal parts.
Twelve-twelfths equals one whole pizza.
The top number in a fraction is called the numerator.
The bottom number is called the denominator.

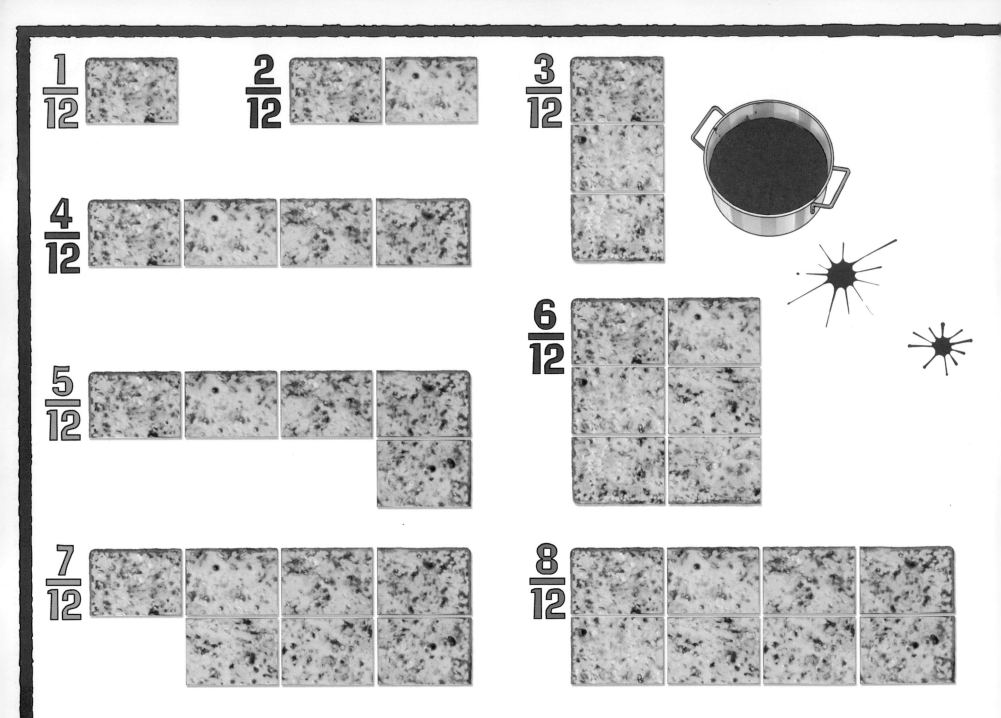

Before we add fractions, let's do a summary.
One-twelfth, two-twelfths, three-twelfths, four-twelfths,
five-twelfths, six-twelfths, seven-twelfths, eight-twelfths,

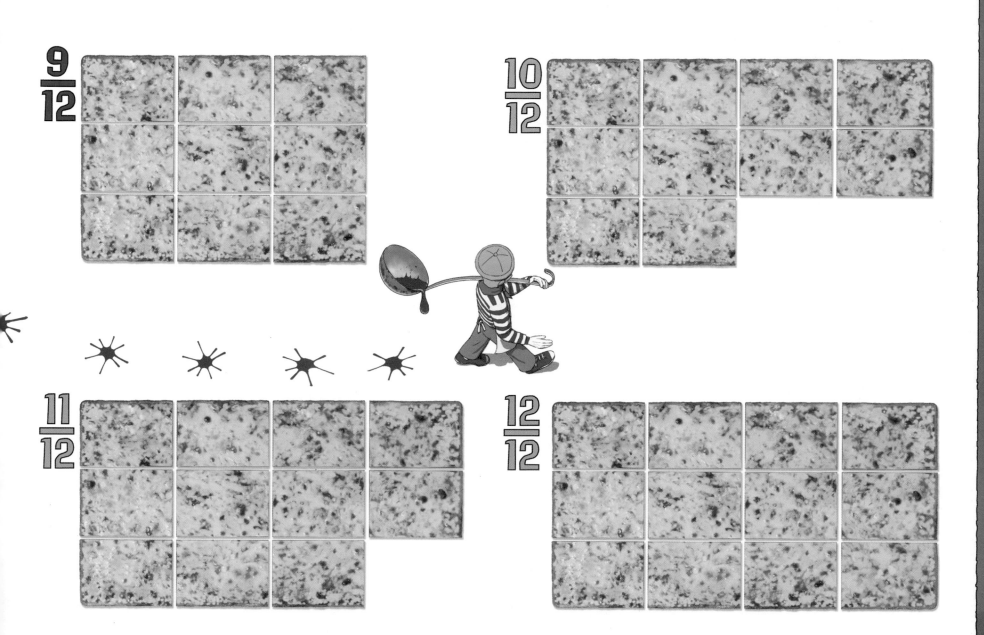

nine-twelfths, ten-twelfths, eleven-twelfths, and twelve-twelfths, which is one whole pizza.

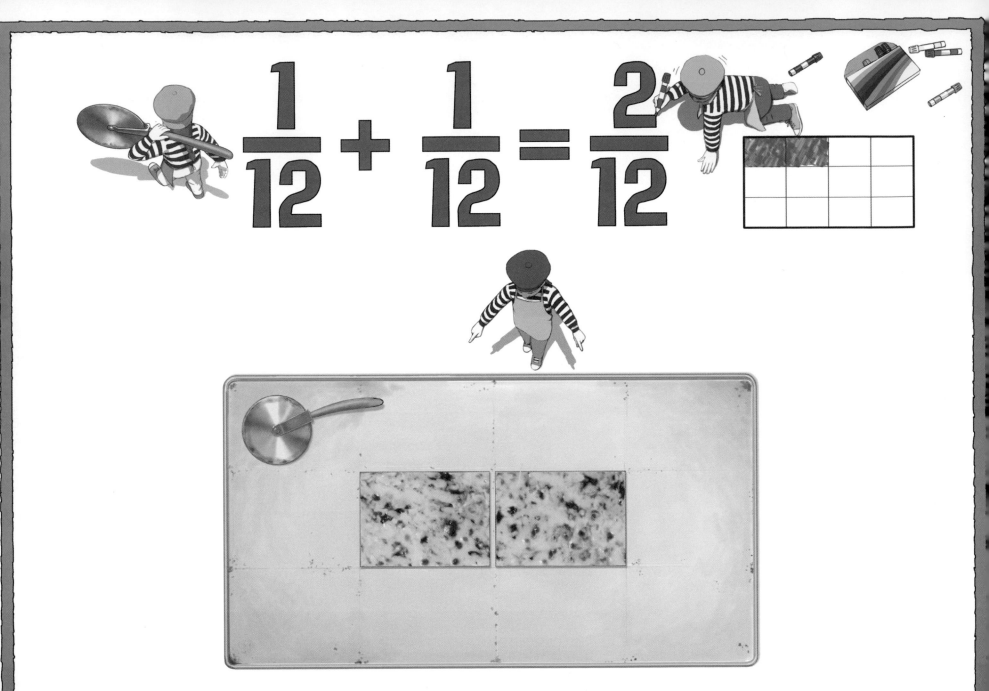

$$\frac{1}{12} + \frac{1}{12} = \frac{2}{12}$$

We are adding only the numerators.
The denominators remain as "twelve."
Now it's time to add some fractions. Here is our first equation.
One-twelfth plus one-twelfth equals two-twelfths.

$$\frac{2}{12} + \frac{3}{12} = \frac{5}{12}$$

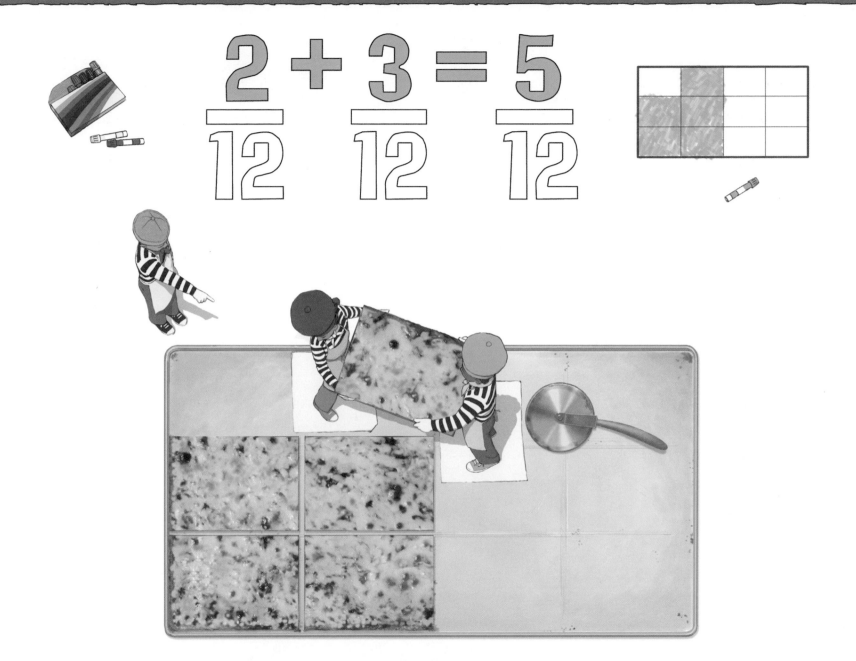

Here is another fraction addition equation.
Two-twelfths plus three-twelfths equals five-twelfths.
Remember, we are adding the numerators.
Adding fractions is easy to do when they have the same denominators.

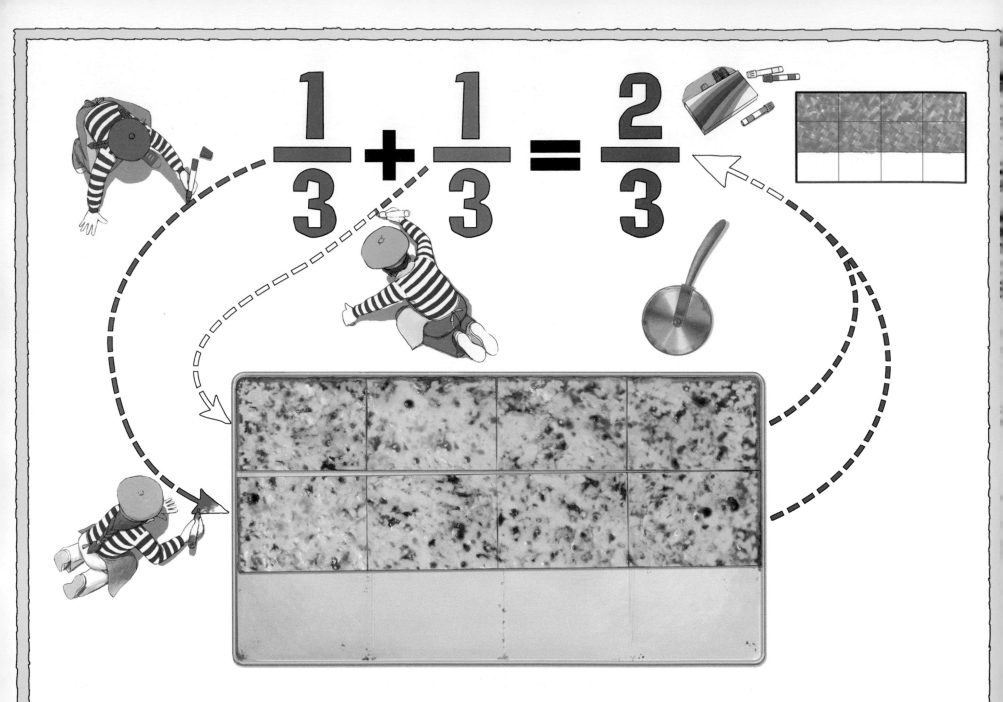

$$\frac{1}{3} + \frac{1}{3} = \frac{2}{3}$$

One-third plus one-third equals two-thirds.
When we add fractions with denominators that are the same,
they are called "like denominators" or "common denominators."

$$\frac{1}{3} + \frac{2}{3} = \frac{3}{3}$$

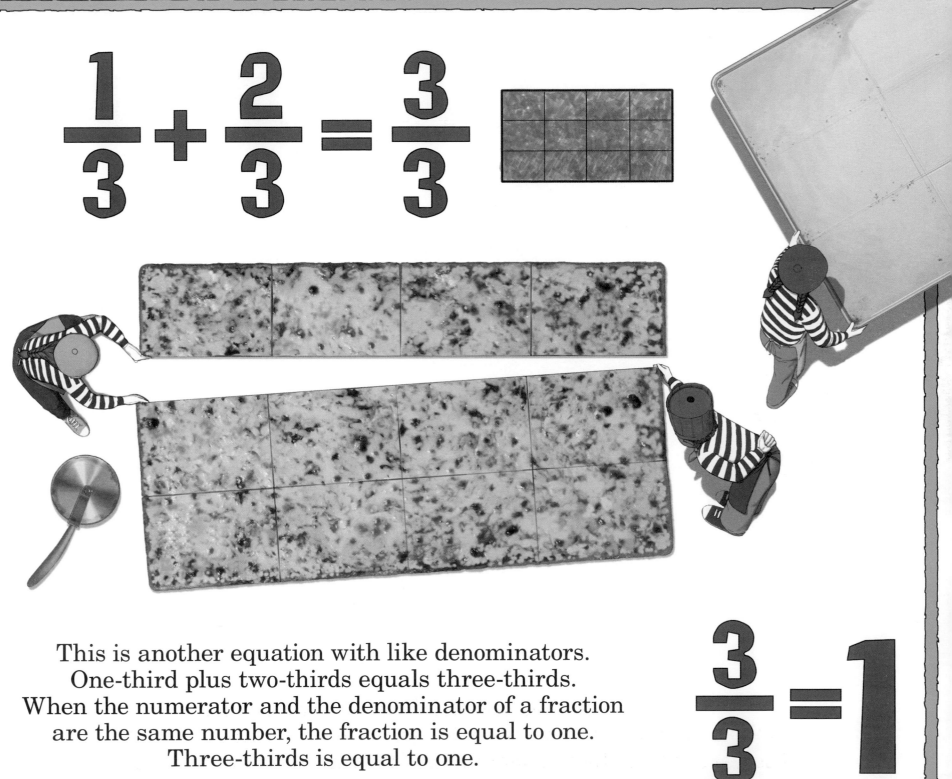

This is another equation with like denominators.
One-third plus two-thirds equals three-thirds.
When the numerator and the denominator of a fraction
are the same number, the fraction is equal to one.
Three-thirds is equal to one.

$$\frac{3}{3} = 1$$

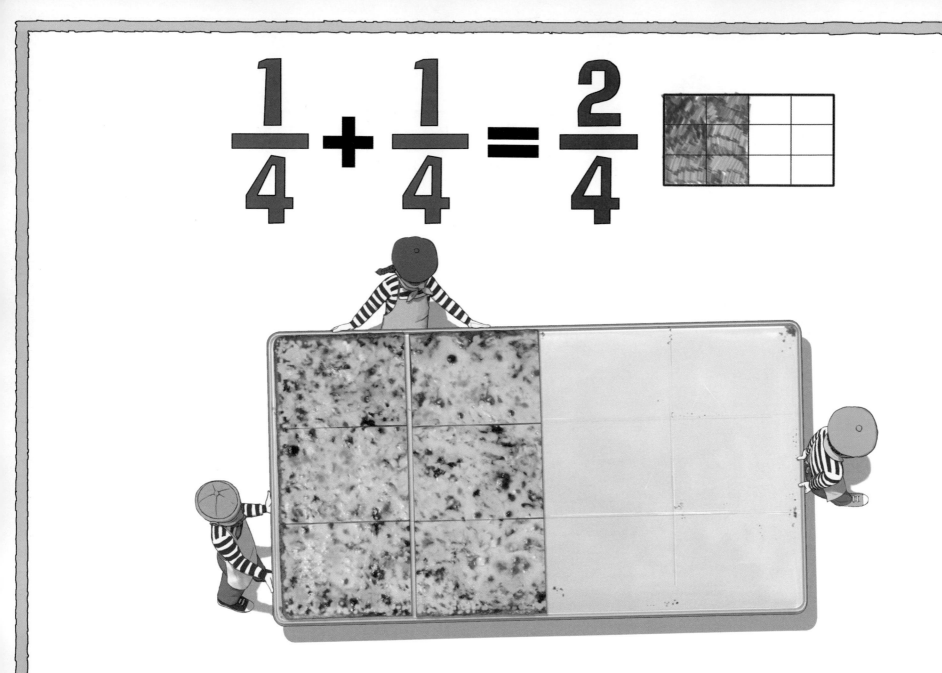

$$\frac{1}{4} + \frac{1}{4} = \frac{2}{4}$$

Now add this equation.
One-fourth plus one-fourth equals two-fourths.
You can see that the fraction two-fourths
is equal to one-half of the whole pizza.

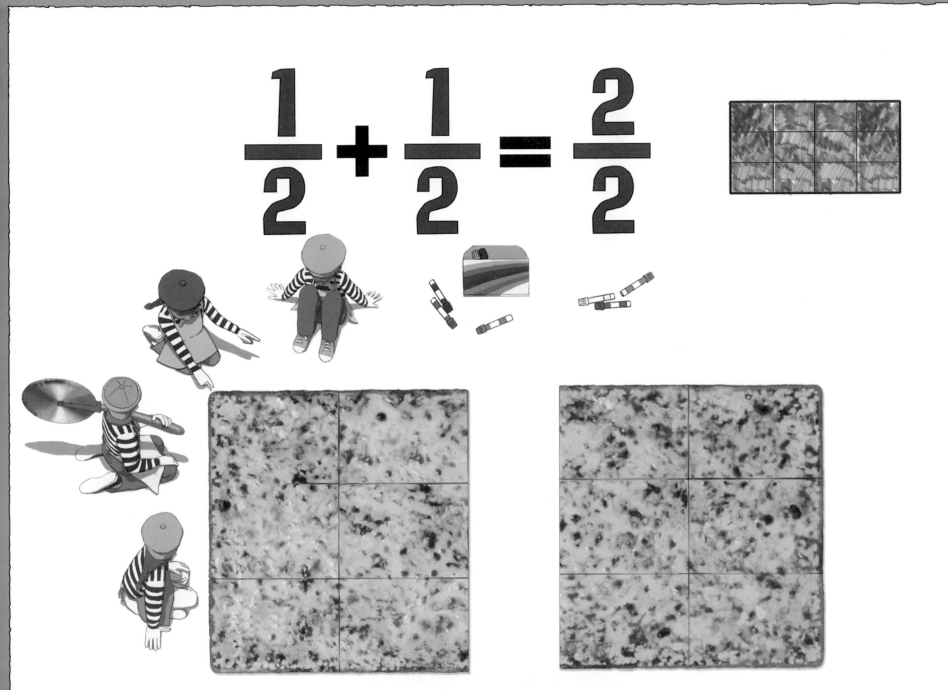

$$\frac{1}{2} + \frac{1}{2} = \frac{2}{2}$$

Here is a new pizza. We simply cut it in half.
One-half plus one-half equals two-halves.
Maybe you have heard the saying: Two halves make a whole!

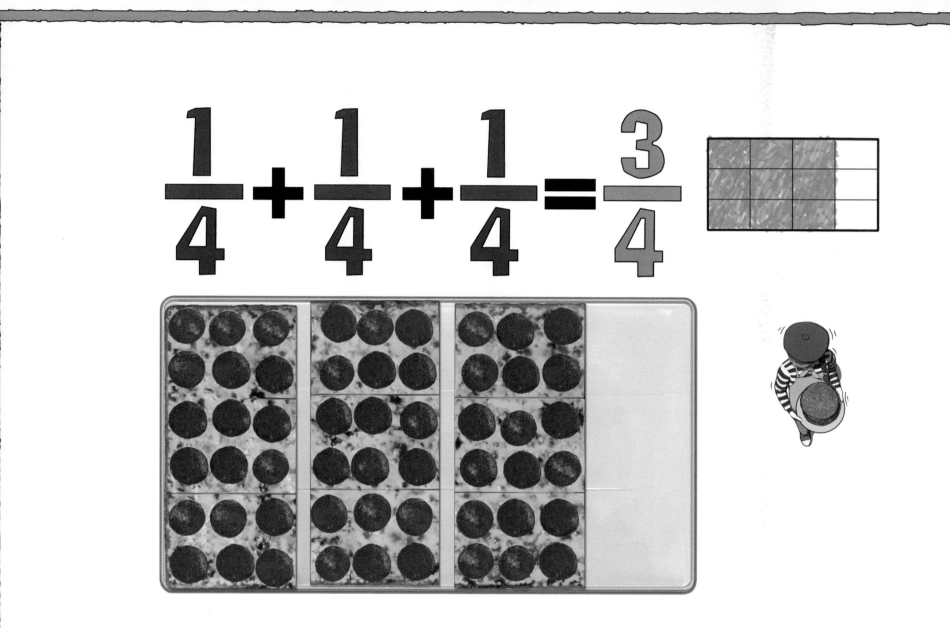

$$\frac{1}{4} + \frac{1}{4} + \frac{1}{4} = \frac{3}{4}$$

Let's try adding three fractions.
One-fourth plus one-fourth plus one-fourth equals three-fourths.
Enjoy the pepperoni!

$$\frac{1}{6} + \frac{2}{6} = \frac{3}{6}$$

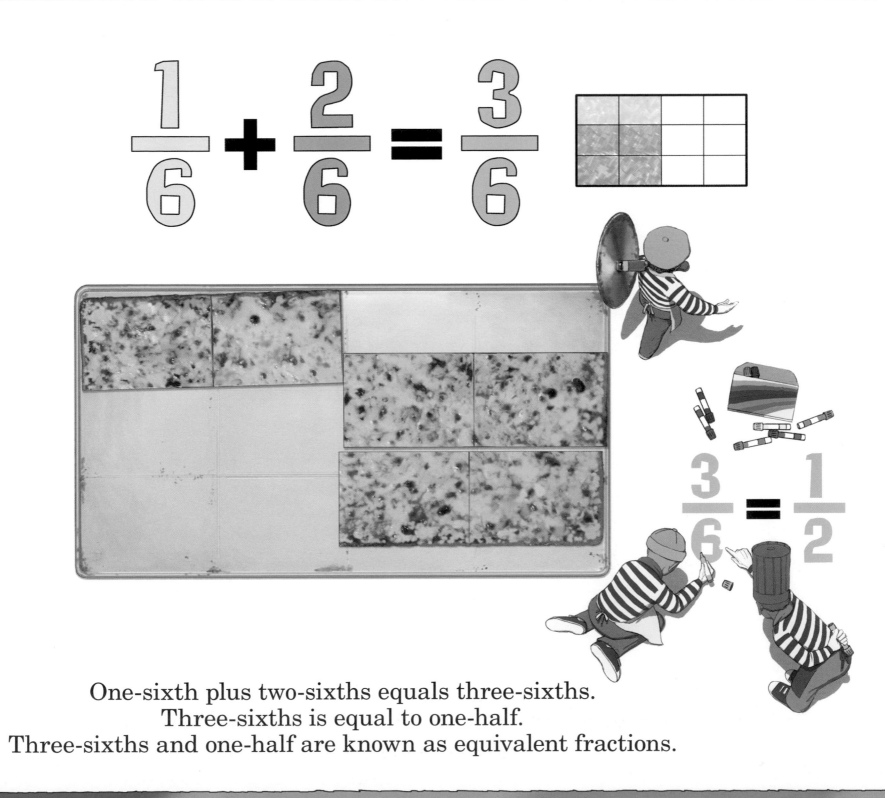

$$\frac{3}{6} = \frac{1}{2}$$

One-sixth plus two-sixths equals three-sixths.
Three-sixths is equal to one-half.
Three-sixths and one-half are known as equivalent fractions.

So far in this book, we have added with like denominators.
Now it is time to add fractions with unlike denominators.
Are you ready?
To add fractions with unlike denominators,
we first need to know their equivalent fractions.

$$\frac{2}{12} = \frac{1}{6} \qquad \frac{3}{12} = \frac{1}{4}$$

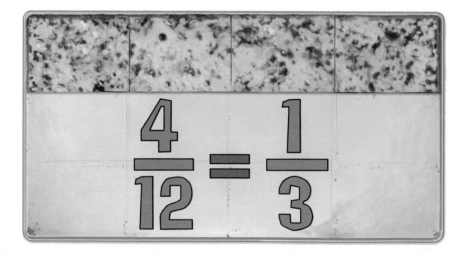

$$\frac{4}{12} = \frac{1}{3}$$

Here is a chart of equivalent fractions.

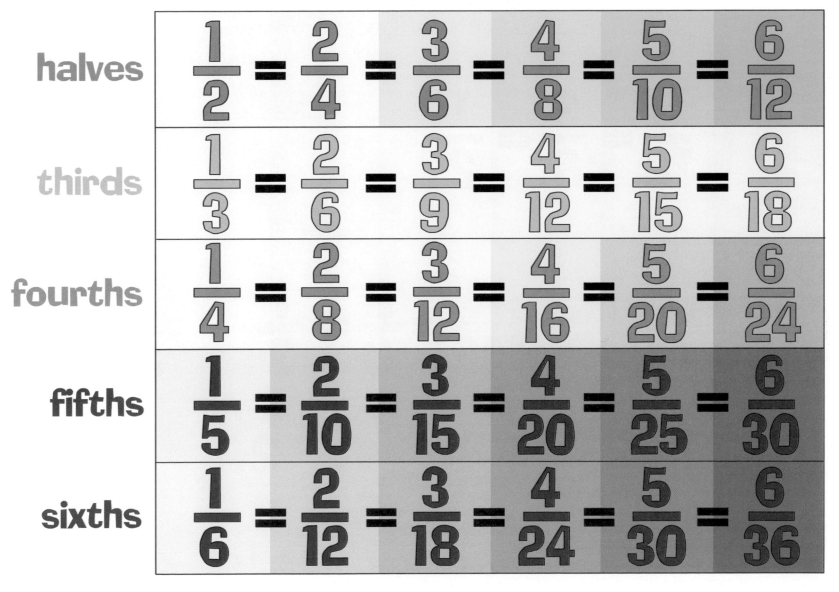

halves $\dfrac{1}{2}$ =	$\dfrac{2}{4}$ =	$\dfrac{3}{6}$ =	$\dfrac{4}{8}$ =	$\dfrac{5}{10}$ =	$\dfrac{6}{12}$
thirds $\dfrac{1}{3}$ =	$\dfrac{2}{6}$ =	$\dfrac{3}{9}$ =	$\dfrac{4}{12}$ =	$\dfrac{5}{15}$ =	$\dfrac{6}{18}$
fourths $\dfrac{1}{4}$ =	$\dfrac{2}{8}$ =	$\dfrac{3}{12}$ =	$\dfrac{4}{16}$ =	$\dfrac{5}{20}$ =	$\dfrac{6}{24}$
fifths $\dfrac{1}{5}$ =	$\dfrac{2}{10}$ =	$\dfrac{3}{15}$ =	$\dfrac{4}{20}$ =	$\dfrac{5}{25}$ =	$\dfrac{6}{30}$
sixths $\dfrac{1}{6}$ =	$\dfrac{2}{12}$ =	$\dfrac{3}{18}$ =	$\dfrac{4}{24}$ =	$\dfrac{5}{30}$ =	$\dfrac{6}{36}$

In this chart, the numbers one, two, three, four, five, and six are used as numerators. The denominators skip count by twos, threes, fours, fives, and sixes.

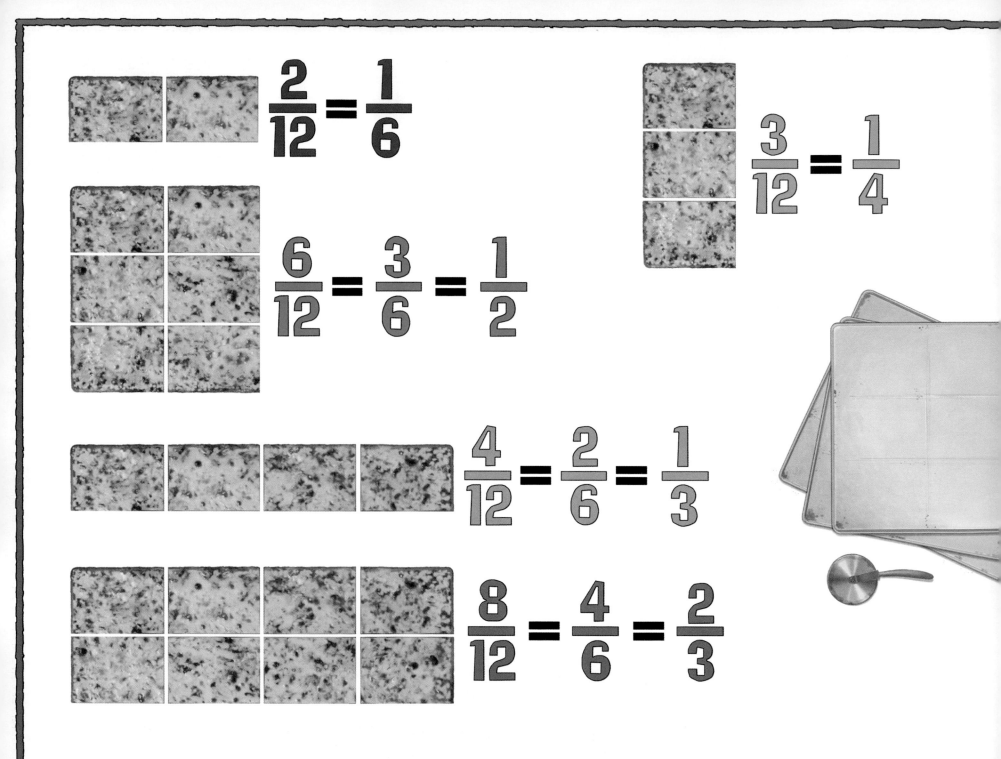

$$\frac{2}{12} = \frac{1}{6}$$

$$\frac{3}{12} = \frac{1}{4}$$

$$\frac{6}{12} = \frac{3}{6} = \frac{1}{2}$$

$$\frac{4}{12} = \frac{2}{6} = \frac{1}{3}$$

$$\frac{8}{12} = \frac{4}{6} = \frac{2}{3}$$

Here is another summary.
This is a summary of equivalent fractions using a twelve-slice pizza.

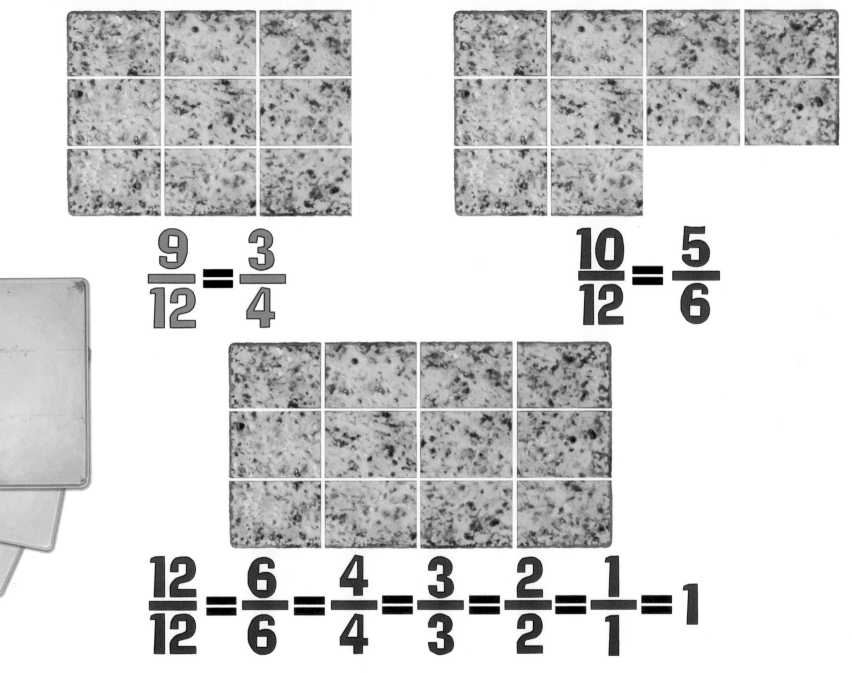

$$\frac{9}{12}=\frac{3}{4}$$

$$\frac{10}{12}=\frac{5}{6}$$

$$\frac{12}{12}=\frac{6}{6}=\frac{4}{4}=\frac{3}{3}=\frac{2}{2}=\frac{1}{1}=1$$

The fractions one-twelfth, five-twelfths, seven-twelfths, and eleven-twelfths are not in this summary. They already have the lowest numerator and denominator possible. They are in their lowest terms.
They do not have an equivalent fraction when using a twelve-slice pizza.

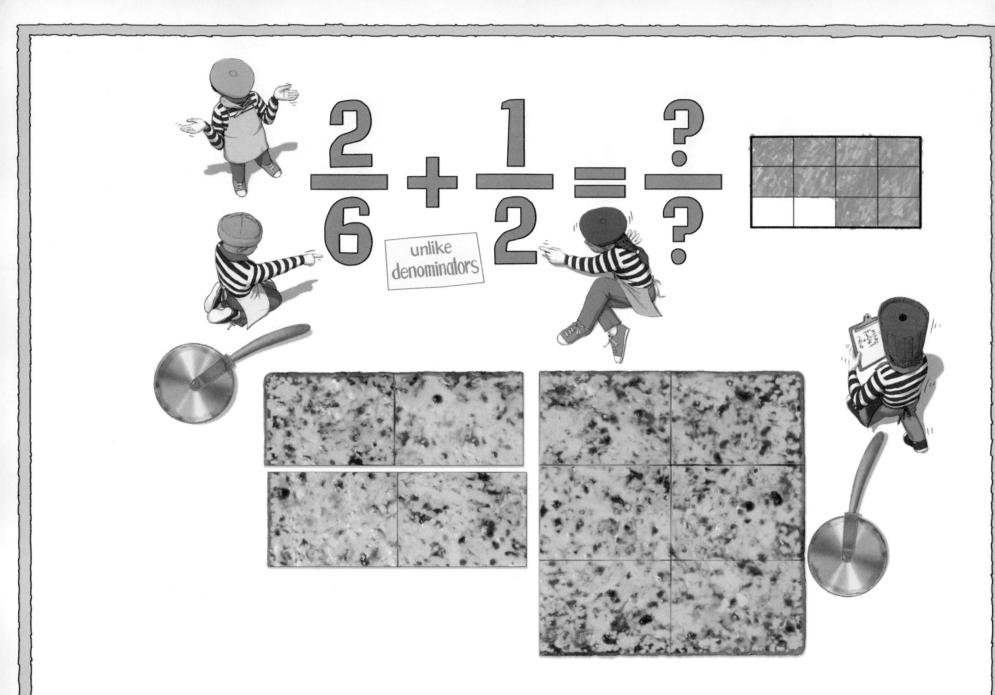

$$\frac{2}{6} + \frac{1}{2} = \frac{?}{?}$$

unlike denominators

Two-sixths plus one-half equals what?
In this equation, the denominator six and the denominator two are different.
We need to have like denominators to add these fractions.

$$\frac{2}{6} + \frac{3}{6} = \frac{5}{6}$$

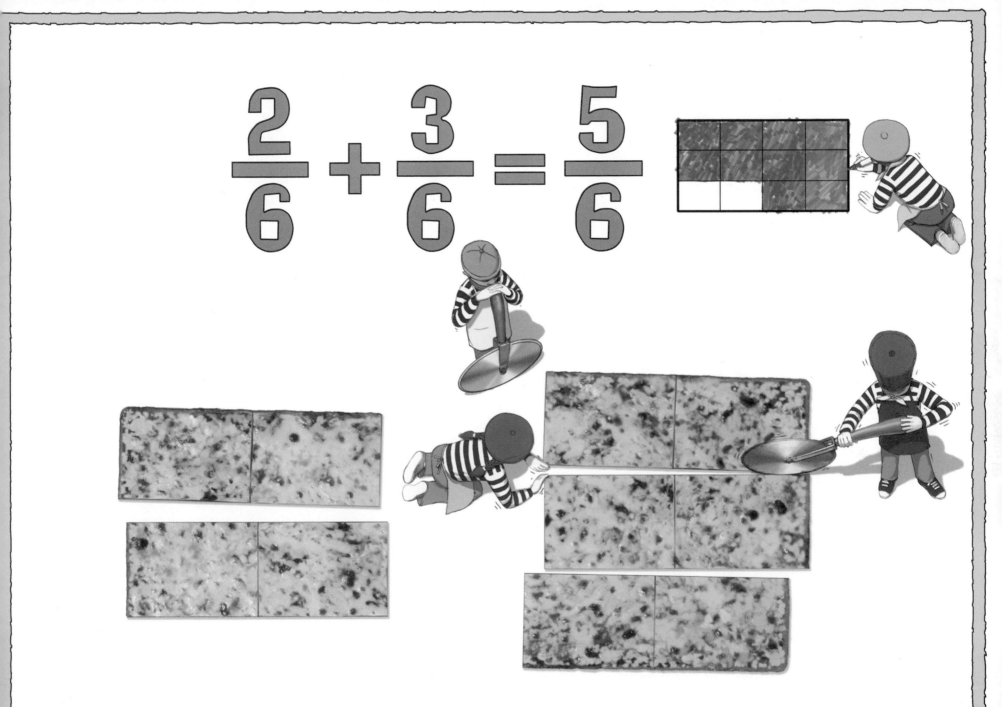

Here is how to do it: Go back and look at the summary of equivalent fractions. Find an equivalent fraction of one-half with a denominator of six. Got it! One-half equals three-sixths. Two-sixths plus three-sixths equals five-sixths.

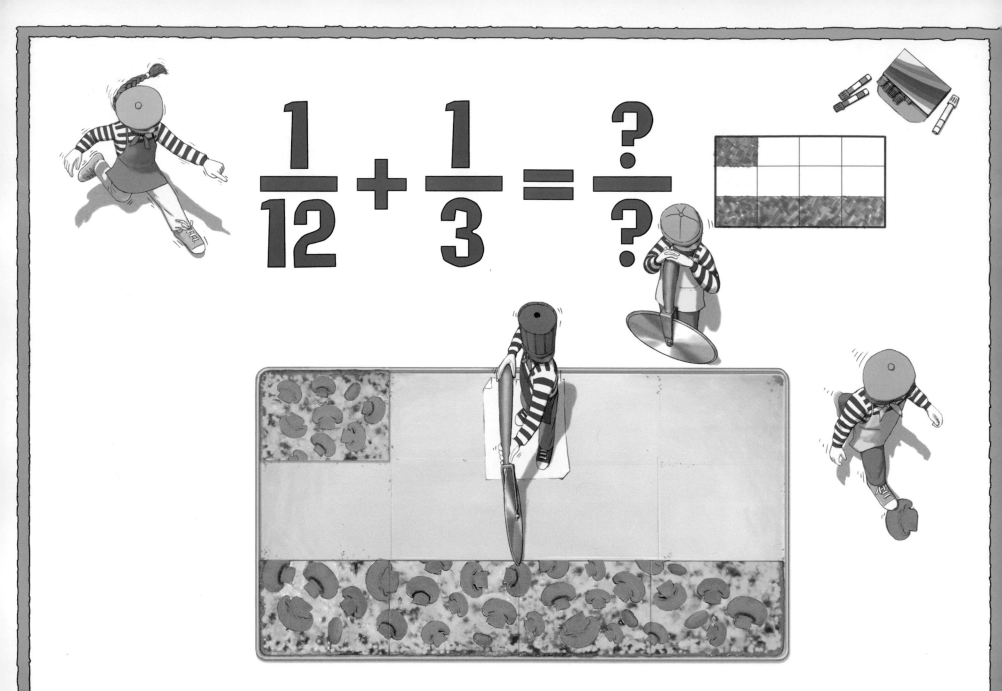

$$\frac{1}{12} + \frac{1}{3} = \frac{?}{?}$$

One-twelfth plus one-third equals what?
What fraction has a denominator of twelve and is equivalent to one-third?
Enjoy the mushroom pizza!

$$\frac{1}{12} + \frac{4}{12} = \frac{5}{12}$$

Four-twelfths is equivalent to one-third.
Now add the fractions. One-twelfth plus four-twelfths equals five-twelfths.
It is the same as saying one-twelfth plus one-third equals five-twelfths.

$$\frac{1}{2} + \frac{1}{4} = \frac{?}{?}$$

One-half of a broccoli pizza plus
one-fourth of a broccoli pizza equals what?
Does one-half have an equivalent fraction
with a denominator of four?
Yes! One-half equals two-fourths.

$$\frac{1}{2} = \frac{2}{4}$$

$$\frac{2}{4} + \frac{1}{4} = \frac{3}{4}$$

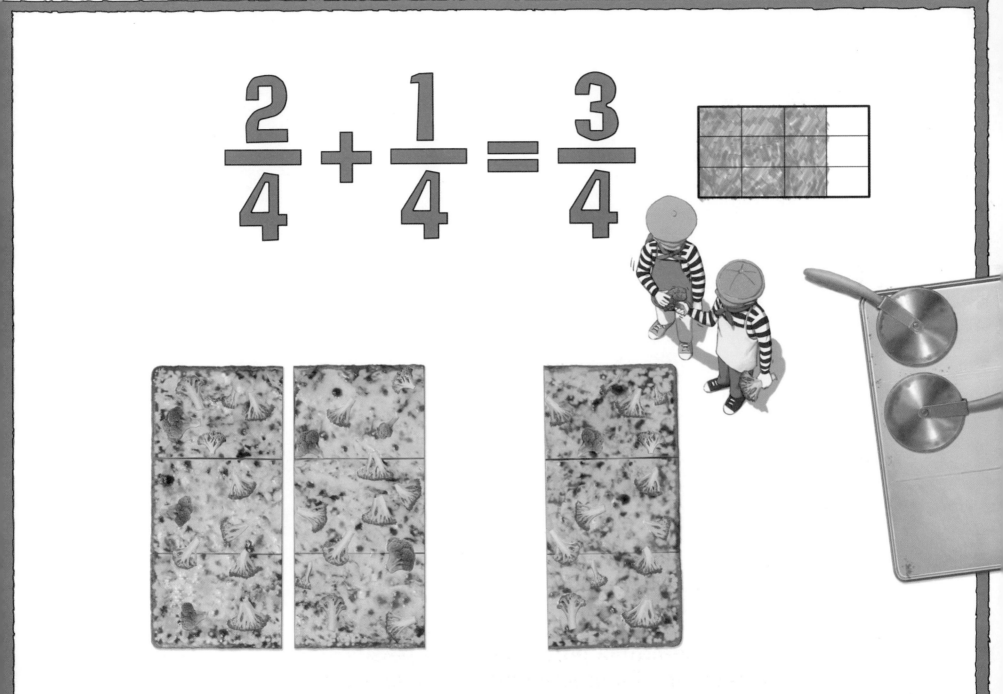

Two-fourths plus one-fourth equals three-fourths.
So, one-half plus one-fourth equals three-fourths!

$$\frac{1}{3} + \frac{1}{4} = \frac{?}{?}$$

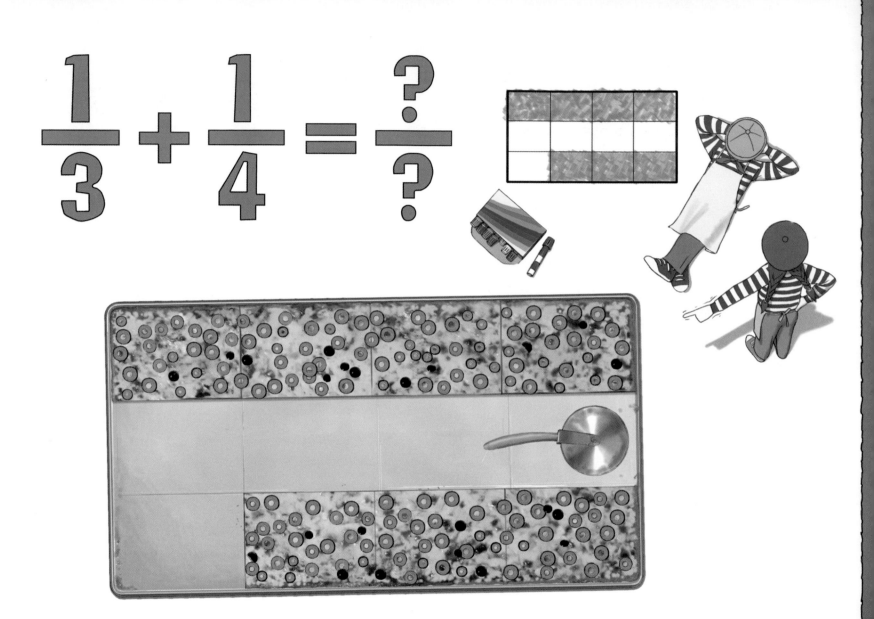

One-third plus one-fourth equals what?
In this equation, to find a common denominator or like denominator,
we have to change both denominators.
One-third is equivalent to four-twelfths.
One-fourth is equivalent to three-twelfths.

$$\frac{4}{12} + \frac{3}{12} = \frac{7}{12}$$

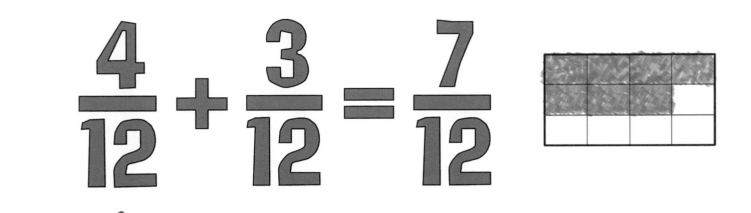

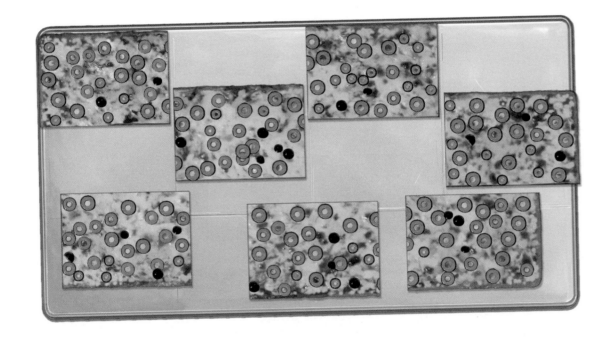

Four-twelfths plus three-twelfths equals seven-twelfths.
Now you know! One-third plus one-fourth equals seven-twelfths.
The illustrator of this book loves olive pizza.

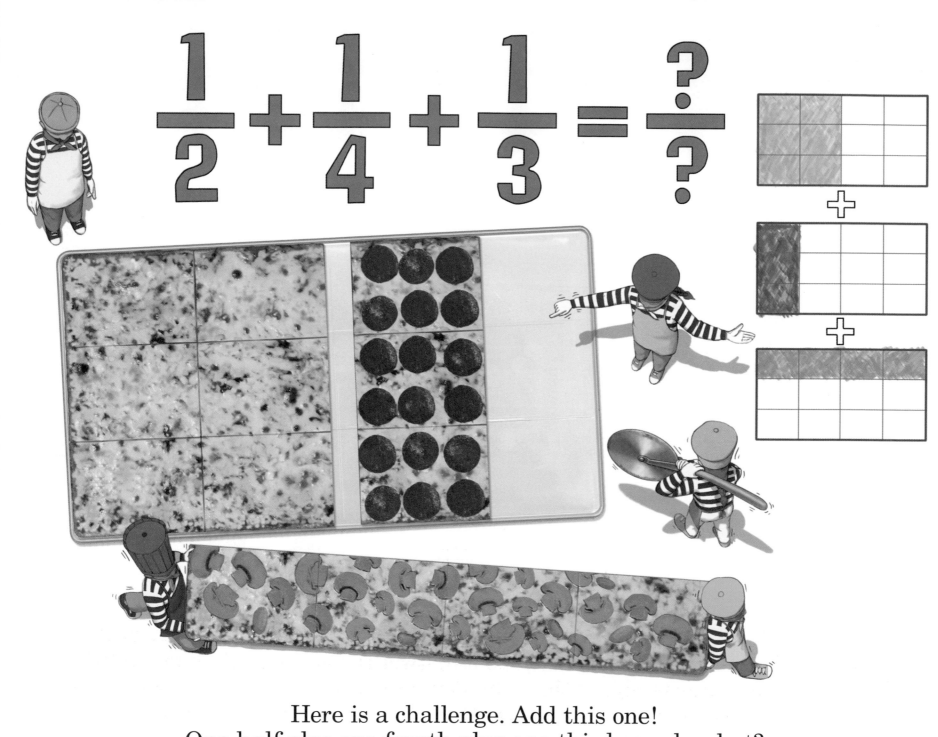

Here is a challenge. Add this one!
One-half plus one-fourth plus one-third equals what?

$$\frac{6}{12} + \frac{3}{12} + \frac{4}{12} = \frac{13}{12} = 1\frac{1}{12}$$

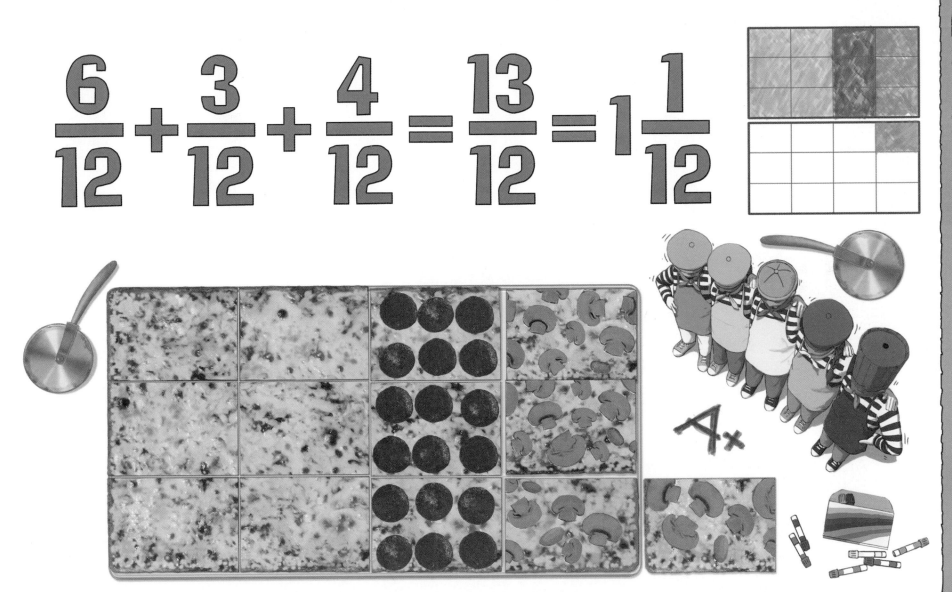

Find the equivalent fractions: One-half is equal to six-twelfths.
One-fourth is equal to three-twelfths. One-third is equal to four-twelfths.
Six-twelfths plus three-twelfths plus four-twelfths equals thirteen-twelfths.
When the numerator is bigger than the denominator, it is an improper fraction.
Thirteen-twelfths is one and one-twelfth. This is known as a mixed number.
We need two pizzas to make thirteen-twelfths.

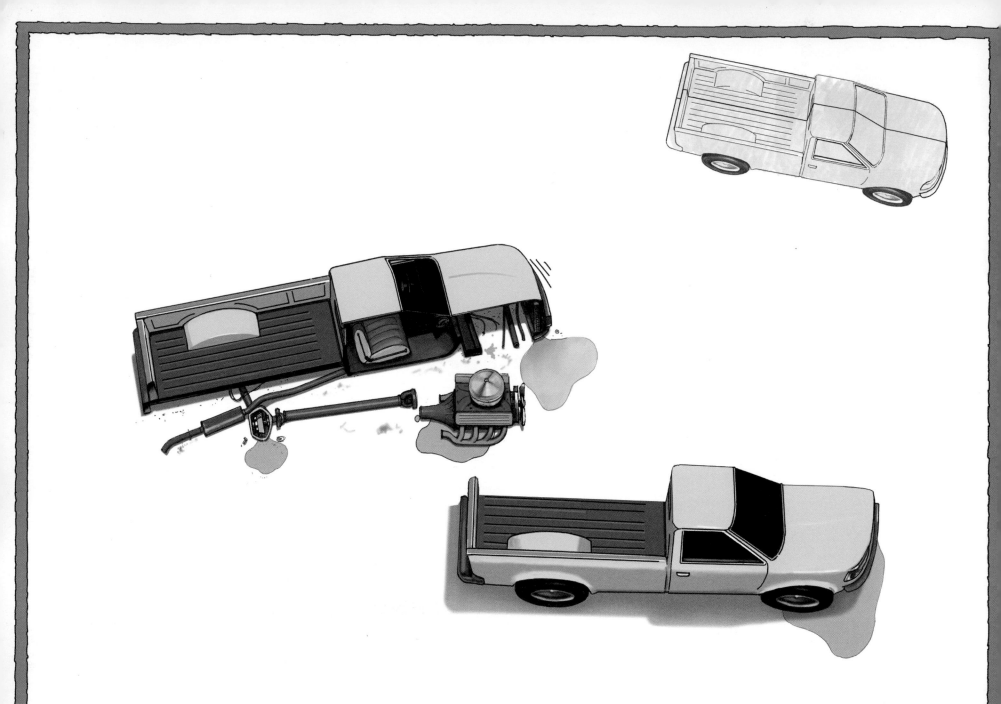

The pizza tasted great.
Aren't you glad we didn't use a pickup truck to teach adding fractions?
It wouldn't fit in the classroom—and who could lift it?